SHARE A STORY

HANDA'S SURPRISE

Introduction

One of the best ways you can help
your children learn and learn to read
is to share books with them. Here's why:

• They get to know the **sounds**, **rhythms** and **words**
used in the way we write. This is different from how we
talk, so hearing stories helps children learn how to read.

• They think about the **feelings** of the characters
in the book. This helps them as they go about
their own lives with other people.

• They think about the **ideas** in the book. This helps
them to understand the world.

• Sharing books and listening to what your children
say about them shows your children that you care
about them, you care about what they think
and who they are.

Michael Rosen

Michael Rosen
Writer and Poet
Children's Laureate (2007-9)

For Emma, Linda, Nadine and Yewande

The author would like to thank everyone who
helped her research this book, especially Wanjiru and
Nyambura from the Kenyan Tourist Office, and
Achieng from the Kenyan High Commission.

The children featured in this book are from
the Luo tribe of south-west Kenya.

First published 1994 by Walker Books Ltd
87 Vauxhall Walk, London SE11 5HJ

This edition published 2011

2 4 6 8 10 9 7 5 3 1

© 1994 Eileen Browne

Concluding notes © CLPE 2011

The right of Eileen Browne to be identified as author/illustrator
of this work has been asserted by her in accordance with the
Copyright, Designs and Patents Act 1988

This book has been typeset in ITC Garamond

Printed in China

British Library Cataloguing in Publication Data:
a catalogue record for this book is available from the British Library

ISBN 978-1-4063-3517-0

www.walker.co.uk

HANDA'S SURPRISE

Eileen Browne

WALKER BOOKS
AND SUBSIDIARIES
LONDON · BOSTON · SYDNEY · AUCKLAND

Handa put seven
delicious fruits in a basket
for her friend, Akeyo.

She will be surprised,
thought Handa as she set off
for Akeyo's village.

I wonder which fruit
she'll like best?

Will she like the
soft yellow banana …

or the

sweet-smelling guava?

Will she like the
round juicy orange …

or the ripe red mango?

Will she like the
spiky-leaved pineapple …

the creamy green avocado …

or the tangy purple passion-fruit?

Which fruit will Akeyo like best?

"Hello, Akeyo," said Handa.

"I've brought you a surprise."

"Tangerines!" said Akeyo.

"My favourite fruit."

"TANGERINES?" said Handa.

"That *is* a surprise!"

banana guava orange mango pineapple avocado pear passion fruit tangerine

Sharing Stories

Sharing stories together is a pleasurable way
to help children learn to read and enjoy books.
Reading stories aloud and encouraging
children to talk about the pictures and join in
with parts of the story they know well are
good ways to build their interest in books.
They will want to share their favourite books
again and again. This is an important part
of becoming a successful reader.

monkey ostrich zebra elephant giraffe antelope parrot goat

Handa's Surprise is a simple yet clever story set in Kenya. For many children it will introduce them to an unfamiliar place with different food, animals and ways of life. Here are some ways you can share this book:

• The book works in different ways with the words and pictures each telling their own story. Talk together about the way the words tell Handa's story while the pictures tell what happened to the fruit.

• The pattern of questions Handa asks herself is quickly remembered by young readers, even if they don't remember the words exactly the first time.

• Through re-reading the story, children will get to know the names of the fruit and animals that are new to them. If they are stuck on a word, encourage them to make a good guess using the pictures. Read it for them if they are really stuck or tired.

• Children will enjoy telling the whole story in their own words, using the pictures to help them.

• Children can make two sets of cards – one with pictures of all the animals in the story, and one with pictures of the different fruit. They can play the "pairs" game, matching the fruit to the animal that eats it. On separate cards, you can then also write the names of the animals and fruit and play another game of pairs, matching the words to the pictures.

SHARE A STORY
A First Reading Programme
From Pre-school to School

Beginnings – 2 years+

Early Steps – 3 years+

Next Steps – 4 years+

Taking Off – 5 years+

Sharing the best books makes the best readers

WALKER BOOKS

www.walker.co.uk